BITTER, OPPRESSED, OR *Blessed*

"Even what was meant to break you can become the very thing that builds you when God gets involved."

CIARA BRILEY

Copyright © 2025 by Ciara Briley
All rights reserved.

No part of this book may be reproduced, stored in a retrieval system, or transmitted in any form or by any means—electronic, mechanical, photocopying, recording, or otherwise—without the prior written permission of the publisher, except for brief quotations used in reviews, articles, or educational settings.

This is a work of nonfiction. The events, conversations, and reflections are based on the author's real-life experiences. Any names or identifying details may have been changed to protect the privacy of individuals.

Cover design, interior layout, and publishing services by:
The 1 and Only Publishing
4500 Forbes Blvd, Suite 200
Lanham, MD 20706
www.the1andonlypublishing.com
First Edition
eBook: ISBN: 979-8-89741-022-4
Print: ISBN: 979-8-89741-023-1

Printed in the United States of America
For permissions, inquiries, or speaking engagements, contact:
The 1 and Only Publishing
info@the1andonlypublishing.com

Ciara Briley
ciarabriley@icloud.com

*To my Father—my Savior, my Lord.
Thank You for being the greatest parent that ever existed. You gave
Your Son and watched Him suffer for sins He did not commit—
willingly, lovingly, and without hesitation.*

*Thank You, Jesus, for choosing the cross and enduring what You
never deserved.*

*Thank You, Holy Spirit, for resting on me, moving through me, and
allowing me to tell this story.*

This book is Yours.

Contents

Prologue: The Mirror Moment..1
Chapter 1: Born into the Storm..3
Chapter 2: Raised by a King 9
Chapter 3: Invisible and Uninvited..15
Chapter 4: A War Within—The Fight to Not Become Her 23
Chapter 5: Running to What I Was Running From...................29
Chapter 6: The Beating That Broke the Illusion 37
Chapter 7: Wings in the Waiting...45
Chapter 8: The Lion and the Butterfly.......................................53
Chapter 9: Delayed but Not Denied 61
Chapter 10: Full Circle Faith 69
Epilogue: The Garden I'm Planting...79

PROLOGUE
The Mirror Moment

I'M THIRTY-SIX YEARS OLD, STANDING IN MY HALF-million-dollar home, holding my miracle baby, and I can still hear those words echoing from my past: *"She's going to end up just like her mama."*

Today, those words make me smile.

Not because they were right, but because they were the fire that forged my wings.

This is the story of how I refused to inherit a legacy of abandonment, addiction, and broken dreams. How I learned that sometimes you have to fly straight into the storm to discover you were built to weather it. How a little girl named Butterfly finally learned to soar.

But first, let me tell you about the day I was born—into chaos, into uncertainty, into a love story that would take thirty-six years to fully understand.

CHAPTER 1
Born into the Storm

"Every butterfly begins its life as something else—crawling, earthbound, invisible. But buried deep within the caterpillar is the blueprint for wings. The cocoon isn't a prison; it's a promise. And sometimes, the most beautiful transformations happen in the darkest places."

Have you ever watched a butterfly struggle to escape its cocoon? No one teaches it how. It doesn't attend a class or take notes. It just breaks free and flies because it must. I think that's why my mother named me Butterfly. Not because she saw beauty in me, but because she knew one day I'd have to survive without instruction, without her.

Even now, I ask myself: How do you become whole when your beginning was abandonment?

They call me Butter for short.

She was just fourteen when she had me. Eight months pregnant, barely past being a child herself, she carried me in her belly and birthed me into a world she hadn't figured out yet. Six months later, she left me at a friend's house and never came back. Said she was going to the store. That was the last time I saw her.

I had to learn to fly on my own.

But let me back up.

I didn't know it then, but that day would echo through every milestone in my life including the day I became a mother.

It was May 16, 1988, in Virginia. The kind of spring day that didn't know what it wanted to be. The air was still cool that morning, heavy with clouds. The kind of clouds that felt more like a blanket than a promise of rain. By afternoon, the temperature crept up fast—86 degrees by the time I took my first breath at 2:29 p.m. The sky remained overcast, a strange contradiction of warmth and gloom, as if heaven itself couldn't decide if my arrival was something to celebrate or mourn.

My mother lay in a stiff hospital bed at Richmond Memorial, tucked inside a cold room with blue and white gowns, blinking monitors, and the scent of sterile chemicals lingering in the air. Her eyes darted between fear and wonder as her contractions grew closer together. Machines beeped. Nurses hovered. An epidural dulled the pain but not the moment. A brown-skinned, brown-eyed girl with a great smile, they said. Beautiful, but "fast," as the older folks used to whisper. That day, she became a mother.

She was ninety pounds before me, 130 with me, trembling in that gown as doctors urged her to push. And push she did; chin to chest, breath held, heart racing. With the fifth push, I arrived.

Bitter, Oppressed, or Blessed

Cries filled the room. Nurses smiled. My mother exhaled like someone who had run a marathon they never trained for. They placed me in her arms. She looked down and said, "My little butterfly."

That was my name before it was ever printed on paper.

The birth certificate came next. Inked footprints of my tiny feet. Thumbprints from my mother. My father's name scribbled in. A 15-year-old boy, trying to be a man. He had caramel skin, light brown eyes, and always dressed sharp. He was the baby of his family, but everyone said he carried himself like the oldest. People knew him. Girls loved him. He had a camera in hand more often than not.

He met my mother at a party. Their first time was quick, she said. But it was enough. Nine months later, I came along.

They tried to hold on. Tried to figure it out. My aunt Bethany watched me sometimes so my mom could catch a breath. My dad brought me a little Coca-Cola onesie for my first photo shoot and took me to Cloverleaf Mall to get my ears pierced. They tried to love me the best way teenagers knew how. But there are things that love can't carry when the people holding it are still growing themselves.

My mother wanted freedom. Weed turned to cocaine, which gave her energy and made her want to be out more and more. Sleepless nights and crying spells wore her thin. One day, she walked into a friend's house with me on her hip and asked their parents if they could watch me while she ran to the store. They said yes.

She never came back.

The couple she left me with didn't know my father. They didn't know the whole story. But they knew love. They took me in like I was their own. Bottles, bedtime, and baby church shoes.

They brought me to Richmond Christian Center each Sunday, nestled in a car seat, as the choir sang and the pastor preached. People assumed I was theirs. No one questioned it. Not really.

Meanwhile, my father kept my baby photo taped in his school locker—me in that Coca-Cola onesie, cheeks full and eyes bright. He hadn't seen me in months. One day, a classmate stopped mid-stride, pointed at the photo, and said, "Yo, my aunt has that baby."

That moment changed everything.

My father tracked the couple down. Showed up at their house. Demanded to take me home. But they refused. They said my mother had left me with them that they were raising me, and they believed it was for a reason.

So my father took them to court. Got a DNA test. And stood in a courtroom, still in high school, asking for his daughter.

The judge looked at him and said, "Not yet."

Told him to finish school first.

The courtroom fell silent.

My father lowered his head, crushed. The couple breathed a quiet sigh of relief. But the clock was ticking.

A year later, he graduated. He came back. This time, the answer was yes.

I was two years old. I had been passed between three different homes and had no idea who my mother was. The couple that loved me had to say goodbye. My father had to give up his dreams of joining the military. He traded his uniform for diapers and bedtime stories.

He chose me.

He took the camera that once chased popularity and turned it toward fatherhood. He took pictures of my first steps, packed lunches, ran bubble baths. He became the kind of father every little girl deserves but rarely gets.

I don't remember those early years. But I remember the feeling that came later the fear that six months would be my breaking point, too. When I gave birth to my own son, I counted down the days until he turned six months old, terrified that I'd feel what she felt: the need to run.

But I didn't.

I stayed.

Because even butterflies have to learn how to land.

And maybe, just maybe, we were born with wings so we could teach the next generation how to fly through the storms we survived.

But staying wasn't the end of the story.

It was just the beginning.

Because the man who fought so hard to save me was about to discover that raising a butterfly meant watching her spread her wings—even when those wings carried her toward danger he couldn't control.

CHAPTER 2
Raised by a King

"They say it takes a village to raise a child, but what happens when the village is just one man with calloused hands and a heart full of dreams he'll never pursue? What happens when a butterfly is raised by someone who's never learned to fly, but refuses to let her crawl?"

THEY SAY NOT ALL KINGS WEAR CROWNS. MINE WORE grease-stained aprons, mismatched socks, and the weight of the world in his silence.

Before we go forward, let's go back for a moment. You've seen the butterfly fly. But let me tell you what it looked like trying to break out of the cocoon—slowly, painfully, blindly emerging.

Sometimes God puts you in the hands of someone who doesn't know they're an angel. Someone who'll sacrifice everything without even knowing they're saving a life.

My father's sacrifice, commitment, and tough love—those weren't just words. They were my life.

First, my dad made his first major sacrifice by joining the military. He had dreams—probably ones he never told anyone about—but he put them aside. After serving, he came home and got approval from the judge to have custody of me.

He came back to Virginia and started working at a restaurant called Darryl's—a popular wood-and-fire grill place off Hull Street. My dad started there as a dishwasher, working in his white shirt with checkered black and white pants. Even while sweating over the grill, he always had a bright smile, cracking jokes and making light of the situation. From dishwasher, he moved to cook. Then manager.

We lived with my grandmother first. But once he saved enough, we moved into our own place—a small apartment complex called Foxwood. Four buildings, one way in and out, located off Snead Road in Richmond, Virginia.

I was five when I first understood sacrifice. Not the kind they teach you in school with crayons and construction paper—real sacrifice. The kind that smells like fried chicken from Darryl's and feels like an empty seat next to you at bedtime. My dad did everything to give me the world, and for a long time, I thought that meant I had everything. Until I realized what was missing. A pocket-sized community with three-story cream buildings, four brick pillars holding up each balcony, and metal staircases that clanged like wind chimes when kids ran up them two at a time. There weren't many swings, just two, and the monkey bars were silver and scraped your palms if you held on too tight.

But we didn't know we lacked anything. It was ours. We were a village.

My dad? He was the center of that world. The man with the booming laugh, flashing white teeth, and a voice that made even discipline sound like a bedtime story. He taught me how to pose, how to throw up a peace sign, how to believe I was beautiful even when no one else said it.

When I got chickenpox, he tried to help me put on my underwear. He couldn't meet my eyes. His face—usually smiling—was frozen, mouth tight, eyes wide, hands fumbling like he was handling something radioactive. Still, he did it. Awkwardly. Gently. Quickly. That was the first time I felt the space between father and daughter widen.

Then came the shoe-tying incident. I stood in the middle of the floor, beads clicking at the ends of my braids, tears balancing on my cheeks. Nessa, the neighbor, knelt beside me. Soft voice. Gentle smile. Freckles like constellations across her cheeks. She didn't laugh. She didn't rush. She just helped.

And I loved her for that.

She felt like the mother I didn't have. My dad noticed, but he didn't say much. Just watched. Quietly.

Then we moved to Town & Country. Just when I was connecting to a mother figure, my father had already made another. It wasn't God's plan for Nessa and me. And maybe it wasn't God's plan for my father and me to stay there either.

Town & Country smelled like fresh grass and chlorine from the pool. To me, it smelled like hope. Like wealth. Like new beginnings. My dad had a new girlfriend, Gina—and she had a daughter. In my eyes, we were becoming a real family. I was finally getting the mother and sister I dreamed of.

For a while, it was magic.

I remember racing the other kids to the pool. My dad standing near the edge, arms crossed, smiling big as I jumped in with no fear. He clapped, proud. For a moment, it felt like we were the Jeffersons—we were moving on up.

Until it wasn't.

Gina didn't want me. I saw it in the way she dressed her daughter in pretty clothes and gave me hand-me-downs. In the way she took pictures of her child standing in the chair and told me to move to the side. I was always the extra. The outsider. The child she never wanted but tolerated because of him.

Still, I stayed silent. I wanted my dad to be happy. He was tired now. His smile faded. His laugh was rare. He came home from work and went straight to bed. No more cookouts. No more neighbors gathered around.

It was like someone had pulled the joy out of him and replaced it with exhaustion. And I was losing him too.

And then came the beating.

It was after I didn't help Gina's daughter fight a boy at the playground. Gina told my father it was all my fault that the incident even occurred. My dad told me to go back outside and kick the boy. The boy had hit my stepsister, and my father—in the only way he knew how to protect us—said, "Kick him back."

So I did.

Later, he held my hand as we walked back to the apartment. I thought maybe he was proud of me. Maybe we were going home to laugh about it.

But when the door closed, the air changed.

He didn't yell. He didn't scold. He just pulled out the extension cord.

I didn't scream. I didn't cry out. I held it all in like I thought I was supposed to. Mouth shut, chin trembling, tears running silently. The bathroom light was on, casting long shadows into the dim room. I remember that light more than the pain.

Later, he tried to rub Vaseline over the welts. His hands shook. His voice cracked. He told me to hush, but I think he was talking to himself.

That night, CPS came.

They asked me if I wanted to stay with him. I didn't think. I didn't hesitate.

Yes.

I had already lost one parent. I wasn't going to lose another.

That night became a turning point—not just for me, but for him. Something shifted. From that day forward, I could feel it: the weight of his guilt, the fear of losing me, the quiet vow to be different. My father once again had a choice to make—me or Gina. And once again, my father chose me.

We moved out of Gina's place into our own apartment one week later.

Three months after we settled in, it was Christmas.

The lights were glowing. The presents were wrapped. I was 75% happy, unlike any kid in a candy store who is 100%. Something was still missing.

My father didn't understand why I was still unhappy. Then he figured it out. He started making calls. He left the house without telling me where he was going.

Then the door opened. Expecting to only see my father—

She walked in wearing a flannel coat and a weathered wrap under a Kangol hat. Her hair was puffed from the humidity. She didn't look glamorous, but I didn't care.

"It's Mommy," she said.

I turned to my dad. His face said it all.

"Yes," he said. "That's your mom."

And I ran to her.

It was the greatest gift I didn't know I could ask for. My mother, wrapped in flannel and hope.

But just like when I was six months old, she didn't stay.

That was the last Christmas we spent in that apartment. The last time I saw her before adulthood. It was the last year of elementary school. The last year of friendships. The last memory I had of fitting in with my peers.

Once again, I was being moved away from the one woman I longed to love.

I thought, now she knows where I am—she can come find me. She promised to come get me and spend time, but that never happened.

And just like that, the tree came down, and the star lost its shine.

People think kids don't notice. That we're too young to understand sacrifice, betrayal, loyalty.

But I did.

I saw a father try to be a king without a kingdom.

I saw a little girl try to be a daughter without a mother.

And somewhere between those two truths, I became a warrior.

But warriors still bleed.

And little girls still break.

Even butterflies bruise their wings while learning how to fly.

And this butterfly wasn't done falling yet.

In fact, the biggest fall was still coming. Because my father was about to make a decision that would take us from the village that loved me to a world where I didn't exist at all.

CHAPTER 3
Invisible and Uninvited

"Sometimes a butterfly finds herself in a garden where her wings don't match the flowers. Where her colors are too bright, too different, too much. But here's what they don't tell you about butterflies: we weren't made to blend in. We were made to stand out. The question is—what happens when standing out feels like dying?"

THE DAY MY DAD PULLED INTO THAT NEW NEIGHBORhood, I thought we had arrived. Paved driveways. Green grass that looked vacuumed. No kids outside, just quiet and space. We weren't in the city anymore—this was the county. My mouth dropped when I saw the house. It was big, almost unbelievable. Four bedrooms. An upstairs and a downstairs. Our own washer and dryer. A pink inflatable couch in my room. And my walls? Sponged light blue, just like I'd asked for. It felt like someone had finally heard me.

I felt like royalty.

But before we even got to this house, there were incidents that sealed our fate—that made my dad realize I was growing up, and boys were starting to notice. My dad wasn't having that.

One incident was on Valentine's Day. A boy from my dance team gave me a teddy bear. I was excited and terrified at the same time. I thanked him but was too scared to bring it home, so I threw it away. But he told someone. That someone told my teacher. And the teacher told my dad.

When I got in the car, he asked, "Where's your bear?" I played dumb, but he knew.

Then came the moment that truly pushed him over the edge. There was this older boy in the neighborhood—a freshman in high school while I was still in elementary. One day he asked for a kiss on the cheek "for luck" during a basketball game. I gave it to him. But my dad found out.

Oh, he was mad. He had that "dad face"—mouth straight, eyes like a lion on the prowl, not blinking, just piercing through my soul. "Don't you ever be out here kissing no dude!" he snapped. "I don't know that boy! He way older than you!" He popped me right there, out of anger and fear.

To make things worse, that same day I had been showing off my outfit—specifically, a skort. I thought it was the coolest thing ever. "Look, y'all! It's a skirt, but it got shorts underneath!" But someone told my dad I was out there "flashing people." I was mortified.

Strike one. Strike two. Strike three. He made up his mind—we were moving.

What I didn't know was that he had already been building a

house in Chesterfield, in a quiet neighborhood called Iron Gate. This house was his dream. And he was making it all work by cutting hair, working nonstop, and sacrificing everything. He even sold his BMW and Jeep to afford this new life. He bought a station wagon and a bike to save on gas.

Oh, I could not stand that station wagon. I was like, "We just got this nice house and you're gonna put this ugly car in the driveway?" It made no sense to me. Everyone else had nice cars, and I thought it didn't belong in the neighborhood.

There are moments that don't just stay in the past—they echo. Not loudly, but like whispers behind closed doors. Like the tension in a house that feels too still. Like walking through a mansion in mismatched shoes. That's what sixth grade felt like: walking into a world that looked like a dream but didn't fit me at all.

It hit like a cold slap. The same clothes I was proud of when I left the house—like my black jumper with Tweety Bird prints—got me labeled instantly. "Baby." "Go back to fifth grade." "You still watch cartoons?"

Every lunch was lonelier. Every hallway walk felt like I was shrinking. I learned fast: they wore Polo and Parasucos. I wore Walmart.

I cried. A lot.

But Daddy noticed.

He held me. Told me it was okay to like what I liked. That I didn't have to change for anybody. But he also scraped together money for a bus trip to New York to buy me the same kind of clothes the other girls wore. Even if they were knock-offs, I finally had a seat at the table.

Sort of.

Because once they decide you don't belong, even a new pair of Jordans couldn't change their minds.

I also realized what having no woman in the house meant when it came to sleepovers. I had a friend who I was excited about—finally somebody I knew who wouldn't outcast me. When I asked her to sleep over, her mom called my dad.

"What other children ought to be there?" her mom asked.

"None, just my daughter."

"How does your wife feel about that?"

"There is no wife."

"So there's no female, no other woman gonna be there?"

"No."

"Okay, no, she's not gonna be able to come. She's not coming over this weekend. She's actually not going to come until there's a woman in that house."

That was the moment of realization.

My dad was working 16-hour shifts—sometimes 12 to 12, 8 to 8. Barely sleeping. Providing for two kids. And we were living in a neighborhood where everyone else had two parents. We stuck out. A Black man and his daughter. Just the two of us.

I started trying to find belonging in the smallest ways.

I skipped class. I did whatever it took to fit in. One time I stole some Jordans from a girl's gym locker. I was so excited because finally people were gonna see I had some Jordans too. But the moment I got caught, I peed myself. I was nervous, terrified. I was a complete wreck—ashamed because one moment I went from Jordans and excitement to no shoes.

There was a boy who lived nearby. I didn't know him well, but I knew enough to know I wanted to feel what the other girls seemed to feel around boys—comfortable, confident, chosen. I didn't like him. I didn't want to date him. I just wanted to be included in something that looked like belonging.

At school, the girls braided the boys' hair like it meant

something. So I offered. Not because I knew what I was doing, but because it gave me a reason to feel seen. He sat on the carpet while I parted and twisted his curls, my hands steady but my heart unsure. I wasn't looking for love—I was looking to not feel invisible.

Someone had been watching from the hallway—quiet, small, and unnoticed. I didn't know he'd seen anything until later, when the truth surfaced. My little brother told on me.

I lied. Said it didn't happen. Said he was making it up. But I could see the disappointment in my dad's eyes—heavy, silent, piercing.

And then came more lies. The permission slips I forged so I could ride in cars with girls who had crews and clout. I wanted to be accepted. I wanted to feel normal. To be chosen.

But every lie stacked like bricks on my chest.

Then came the incident with the underwear.

It was early morning. I had just started my period but didn't know what to do. I had already messed up my own underwear and in panic, I grabbed a pair of my brother's. Pulled them on. Ran to catch the bus.

I buried them in the laundry later, hoping no one would notice. But my dad found them.

He begged me to tell the truth. He was scared—wondering if something had happened to me. Or if it was just nature. I kept lying.

Finally, he gave up. He knew the truth.

He didn't yell. He didn't curse. He didn't hit.

He just looked through me.

That kind of stare that makes your bones go cold. Then he walked out onto the porch like a man unraveling.

He didn't know what to do with me.

So I started skipping class. Slipping through the cracks, hiding in plain sight. I didn't fit in with the girls at school, and I didn't fit in with myself either. Every day felt heavier than the last, like I was walking through fog no one else could see.

My father noticed, but he didn't know what to do with me. After the lies, the silence, and now the skipping, he was running out of options. So he took me to juvenile hall. He thought maybe if I saw where I could end up, it would scare me straight.

Steel benches. Walls that hummed with pain. Kids with eyes too old for their faces. I sat there in silence, watching them, wondering if I belonged. Deep down, I knew I didn't. But for a moment, I thought he might leave me there anyway.

We left, but nothing changed.

I didn't talk about it. He didn't either. We both just moved through the days like shadows in the same house.

After that, he started coming home earlier. Didn't say much. But I'd find my favorite snacks on the counter. He would leave pads on the counter without a word. He was trying to reach me in the only ways he knew how.

He couldn't understand who I was becoming. And truthfully, neither could I.

So I shut down.

I stopped speaking. Not just out of anger. Not to punish anyone. But because my voice didn't feel like it mattered anymore. Everything I said was wrong, misunderstood, or used against me.

So I let silence speak for me.

I took a sheet of paper. Ripped it. Over and over. The sound was the only thing that calmed me. Tearing pages felt like control.

My dad called it a breakdown.

This time, he did leave me. He checked me into the psych ward. It was cleaner than juvy. Quieter. I recognized a girl from elementary school. She looked like a mirror—exhausted, floating, half there.

They gave me Zoloft. I wanted it. I wanted the silence in my head to soften.

But my grandma said no.

"All you need is God," she told me.

She meant well. She always did. But her words landed like a challenge:

Be strong. Be still. Be better.

So I tried.

But trauma isn't linear.

A few weeks after my release, I ran into one of the girls from juvy outside a gas station. I recognized her right away, but I could tell by her face that she hadn't forgotten me either. Her eyes narrowed like I owed her something. "You were just on a tour," she snapped. "You think you're better than us."

I didn't even get the chance to explain. To say I never thought I was better than anyone. To say I was just trying to survive.

She didn't hesitate.

Before I could back away, her fists were swinging. Others joined in. It all happened so fast.

White jeans. Red sweater. Black asphalt. My back hitting concrete. My vision blurring. Their laughter slicing through me sharper than any punch. Cars passed. No one helped.

I didn't fight back.

Because I was more afraid of what my father would say than of the girls hitting me.

Eventually, I ran. Wind screaming in my ears.

I opened the front door. Locked it behind me. Leaned against the wood, chest heaving. Collapsed to the floor, knees to chest. Trying to disappear.

And in that moment, part of me wished I would.

Looking back now, I wish I could grab that girl by the hand and whisper, "You are more than this."

I'd tell her the nerds end up winning.

That she is wonderfully made.

That the girls laughing now won't even matter later.

That joy is still coming.

That God didn't forget her.

That even bruised butterflies still rise—tattered, trembling, but determined.

And if the shoes don't fit the house, kick them off and keep walking.

Because your wings were never meant to blend in with the ground.

They were born to disturb the sky.

But before I could learn to soar, I would have to face the words that would either destroy me or forge me into something unbreakable. Words that would echo in my mind for years: "You're gonna be just like your mama."

The war for my soul was about to begin.

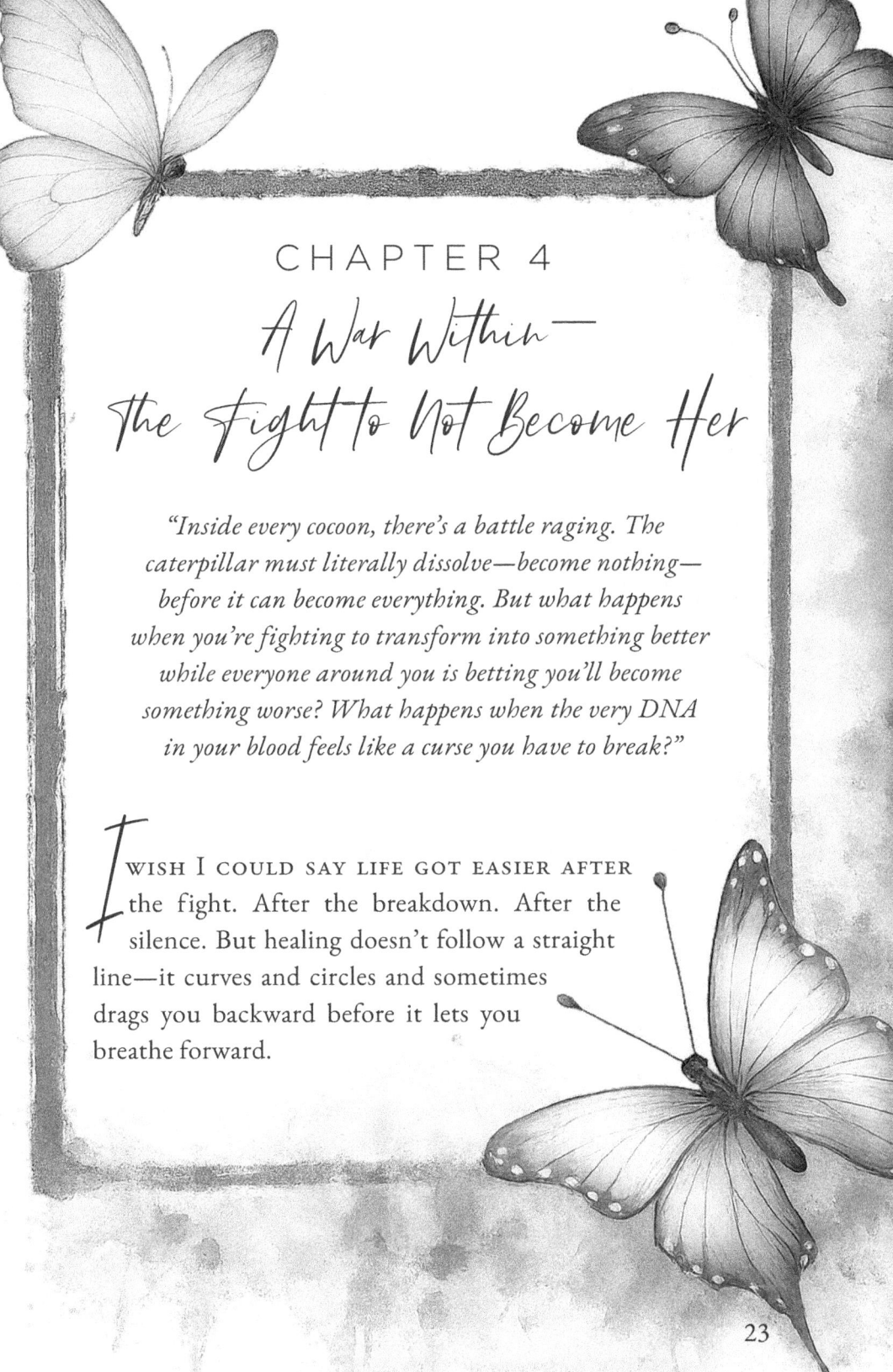

CHAPTER 4

A War Within— The Fight to Not Become Her

"Inside every cocoon, there's a battle raging. The caterpillar must literally dissolve—become nothing— before it can become everything. But what happens when you're fighting to transform into something better while everyone around you is betting you'll become something worse? What happens when the very DNA in your blood feels like a curse you have to break?"

I wish I could say life got easier after the fight. After the breakdown. After the silence. But healing doesn't follow a straight line—it curves and circles and sometimes drags you backward before it lets you breathe forward.

When I transferred schools, I hoped it would be a fresh start. A quiet place to figure myself out. I had no idea it would become the backdrop for one of the most important shifts in my story.

The school was small. Not just in size, but in energy. It was much smaller—maybe a third of the size of the school I was in before. Where the previous school might have had 25 to 30 kids in each classroom, these classrooms had maybe seven kids, 10 at the max. The whole purpose was to have more individual attention for each student. Gone were the crowded hallways and the swarm of judgmental eyes. This place felt more like a whisper than a shout. No one was performing, pretending, or posturing for attention. There was just space—space to breathe, to ask questions, to not know the answer and not feel ashamed of it. For the first time in a while, I didn't feel like I was in survival mode. It felt safer.

It reminded me of where I came from. Not the chaos or the trauma, but the closeness. The simplicity. The quiet way a person could just be without having to earn it.

I was beginning to settle in. I felt a new rhythm building, a soft peace taking root. But just as I started to believe that maybe—just maybe—I could begin again, the past tapped me on the shoulder.

Gina—my brother's mom—delivered the blow.

"You're gonna be just like your mama."

I don't remember what I did to spark it. Maybe I was too loud. Maybe I rolled my eyes. Or maybe I was just becoming a teenager, and that was threat enough.

But what I heard was: you're going to be nothing. You're going to mess up. You're going to fall in line with every broken prediction laid before you.

Something in me clenched.

Oh yeah? Bet I won't.

That moment became fuel. I didn't want to live in the projects forever. I didn't want to be passed around from house to house. I didn't want my name to be tied to pity, disappointment, or a long list of what-ifs.

And then, for the first time in years, I went to visit her—my mom.

Her apartment was small, cement walls and a heavy brown metal door. It smelled like fried chicken and survival. She didn't look like a crackhead. At least not like the ones you see on TV. She looked like a woman trying to keep it together.

She showed me off. To every neighbor, every friend she passed. "This is my daughter. Don't she look good? She ain't got no kids. She doing good in school."

She paraded me like I was proof she'd done at least one thing right.

And in that moment, I felt seen.

Not for what I did wrong, or who I might become, or what rules I'd broken. Just for existing. Just for being hers.

Then came the moment I still can't forget. We were sitting around, and she pulled out some weed. I remember the way she handed it to me like a gift. She didn't say much, just, "Don't tell your daddy."

And I didn't.

Was it wrong? Maybe. I knew it wasn't normal. But it was a moment. A shared experience. Something that was *ours*. It didn't matter whether it was right or wrong—it was ours. And for the first time, I felt like we had a memory that belonged to just us, not a story told about me, but one I was finally part of.

When I came back home, it was like I had new eyes. I started paying attention—not just to what was said, but to what wasn't. Every light left on. Every dish in the sink. All the little things my father used to scold me for, he was doing too. One night, I turned off the bathroom light and left the door open. It wasn't rebellion—it was a signal. My small way of saying, 'I get it now. I'm trying.'

But it didn't land that way.

Instead, he accused me of stealing change from his drawer. And maybe I had before. A few coins here and there. But that night, I hadn't. That night, I was trying.

That was the thing about my father. When I was good, he praised me. When I messed up, the love felt like it vanished. There wasn't much middle ground.

Punishment came swiftly and stayed long. Weeks turned into months of silence, of being grounded with no connection to the outside world. My room became my whole universe—Bible open, schoolbooks stacked, and a Mary Mary CD called "Thankful" looping like a mantra. I played it so much the lyrics began to sound like my own heartbeat, echoing the prayers I didn't yet know how to speak.

In that stillness, something in me started to burn. Not with anger, but with resolve. I couldn't rewrite where I came from, but I could decide where I was going. So I started making vows—not out loud, not on paper, but deep in my spirit:

No babies before marriage. No drugs up my nose. No becoming the version of my mom that people whispered about in pity.

School became my battleground and my escape. I chased straight A's like they were oxygen. Because if I couldn't control anything else, I could at least control that. I could become the girl no one expected—and everything they said I couldn't be.

And then, all that quiet determination paid off. I did it—I graduated early. Straight A's. Walked across the stage with my whole family cheering like I'd just won an Olympic medal. My father showed up in a pink linen suit with a white hat and matching pink sunglasses, loud and proud. For once, I didn't feel like a background character. That moment? That was pride. That was proof that I could rewrite the story.

But college... that was another story entirely. I thought walking across that stage meant I was ready for the world—that academic success would translate into life skills. But as soon as I stepped onto that campus, everything shifted. It felt like entering a foreign country with no language, no guidebook, and no familiar faces.

The classrooms were massive. The expectations, even bigger. And me? I shrank. I felt invisible in crowds, lost in lecture halls. No one told me where to go for books, how to register for classes, or what questions to ask. I wasn't dumb—I had the grades to prove it—but I felt illiterate in this new world. Unprepared. Alone.

So I drifted. Started partying. At least there, no one expected me to have it all figured out. The music drowned out the pressure. The people didn't care if I had the answers. They just wanted to dance.

But the parties ended.

And when the music stopped, I was still empty.

Eventually, I hit bottom. But I didn't know it was the bottom until I tried to come home.

I knocked on my father's door, high, broken, reaching.

He looked at me like I was a stranger.

"No," he said, almost laughing. "You must've forgot who I was."

And just like that, the one place that had always been mine was gone.

It felt like God Himself had turned me away.

I believed the lie right then: *My father doesn't love me anymore.*

So I went looking for someone who would.

I went to find my mother again.
Not for healing. Not for closure.
Just for a place to belong.

But sometimes, when you're desperate enough to be loved, you'll fly straight into the fire thinking it's the light. And I was about to discover that the woman who gave me life was living in a world that could take it away.

The butterfly was about to enter the spider's web.

CHAPTER 5
Running to What I Was Running From

"There's a moment in every butterfly's journey when she realizes the very flower she thought would give her nectar is actually poisonous. But by then, she's already landed. By then, she's already tasted the sweetness that hides the bitter truth. The question becomes: will she have enough strength left in her wings to fly away?"

What happens when the place you thought would save you becomes the very thing that breaks you? What do you do when your search for safety leads you straight into the arms of the danger you thought you left behind? I used to think home was a place—four walls, a bed, someone who calls you "baby." But I learned that sometimes, home is just the last door that opened when every other one slammed shut.

I didn't go looking for my mother—I crashed into her like a last-ditch prayer. After my father shut the door in my face—high, broken, and begging for grace—I ran. Not toward healing. Toward history. Toward the only woman I thought might still open the door.

At the time, I was in a place of transition—trying to get another apartment, bouncing between my grandmother's house and sleeping in my car. I had just gotten a job, but what I really wanted was freedom. So, I left my grandmother's and reached out to my mom.

When she did, her face lit up like I was everything she'd been waiting for. "Come on in, baby," she smiled. "This is your home too." It was the opposite of what I'd just experienced. Where my father's silence felt like a sentence, my mother's embrace felt like a pardon. And for a moment, I let myself believe I'd found safety—that maybe, just maybe, this was the kind of love that would stay. That the arms that opened the door would be the same ones to hold me through the wreckage.

My mother was living in the projects on the North Side, in a two-bedroom apartment. She lived with her boyfriend and my younger brother—her son, not my dad's. His name was Marquis.

My mom said, "Come on, move in with me."

I was hesitant. "I'm not going to be here long. I'm just saving up for an apartment."

She insisted, "Come on, come on, come on."

So I did. I brought what I had—my mattress, my clothes—and moved in. My little brother Marquis gave up his room so I could have it. He said, "I'll just sleep in the living room."

That shocked me. The level of acceptance after years of rejection was awesome.

Her place was small and crowded. Cement walls. A rusted lock on the door. But it didn't matter. I wasn't looking for luxury. I was looking for belonging. My brother greeted me like we'd grown up side by side. No judgment, no hesitation. Just love. That welcome settled something in my chest.

But almost immediately, things felt... off.

People came and went constantly. Strangers knocking at all hours. She'd say she'd be right back and disappear for who-knows-how-long, returning with a different energy—sometimes hyper, sometimes silent. At first, I ignored it. I wanted to keep the picture whole. I wanted to pretend this was the version of motherhood I'd always been missing.

Then she told me she was proud of me.

And I believed her. For a second, I felt like I'd won something. Like I had finally proven I wasn't broken. That I was worthy. It didn't register yet that her version of "proud" was rooted in survival. That finishing high school and not having a baby was the ceiling of her hope. I didn't see then that my father and mother held two entirely different measuring sticks. To him, I hadn't gone far enough. To her, I'd already gone too far.

She showed me off around the neighborhood. "This my daughter," she said. "Her daddy might not be feeling her, but I got her now. He did what he could, but now it's my time to turn her into the woman she needs to be."

I wasn't there to prove anything. I just wanted a relationship. A mother. A bond. Even if it was just for a season. For three months, I tried to belong.

We spent a lot of time together—eating crab legs bought with her food stamps, going to parks with my little brother, watching movies. We smoked together, we drank together. We laughed. It felt like the bond I had always dreamed of.

That meant doing whatever it took to stay in her good graces. Drinking with her. Smoking. Even popping pills. One day she offered me a Xanax. "This'll make you feel better," she said. I took it. That one pill turned into two. Then three. Then more. I started numbing myself—missing my dad, missing stability. But I told myself this was better. This was connection. At first, it felt like bonding. Later, it became a way to bury the truth I couldn't ignore. Because what I'd pushed aside—her disappearances, the strangers, the mood swings—started pressing in.

Then one day, I opened the wrong closet.

Guns. Wads of money. FBI gear. Drugs. The kind of stuff you see in movies, not in your mother's house. My breath left my body. I couldn't move. Couldn't speak. I just stared, frozen, like maybe if I didn't blink, none of it would be real.

But it was real.

That same day, while I was cleaning, the crack of gunfire split through the air. One shot struck the floor just feet from where I stood. I didn't flinch. Didn't scream. My body had already surrendered to the numbness. I moved like a ghost, disconnected from fear, from instinct. When my brother looked at me and said, "Relax, we got you," it didn't sound like comfort—it sounded like a warning. Like I had stepped into something I couldn't step out of.

Then came the moment that broke something in me: a roach floated up in my soda can. I had left my soda on the table, fell asleep, woke up and took a sip—and gagged. I flinched, horrified, but my mother laughed.

"That's normal," she said. "That's something you supposed to know. How you don't know that?"

Like I was stupid for not knowing. Like disgust was a luxury. Like this was just how things were. It was definitely a new low, realizing this was an everyday thing for her.

After that, everything spiraled. My car wasn't mine anymore—it became a family vehicle. I had to schedule fake errands just to get out of the house. When my mom pushed me to go on a date with one of her friends, I said yes. Not because I wanted to, but because I was afraid that saying no would make her stop loving me.

What I thought was just a simple ride—an awkward favor disguised as a date—quickly unraveled into something darker. That 'date' turned into a drug run.

I sat next to a man making deals in parking lots, terrified I'd be arrested. When my mom came back to the car, smiling like nothing happened, I didn't feel safe—I felt used.

The final straw came after a trip to Miami. My friend and I had planned it as a quick getaway, a break from the heaviness that had settled over everything. But things fell apart quickly—we didn't manage our money well and found ourselves stranded. In desperation, we ended up stealing a suitcase off the baggage carousel. The tags were still on, and everything inside was brand new. We told ourselves it was harmless, maybe even karma in our favor. We pawned the contents just to afford a bus ride home.

When I walked back through the door, the air felt off. My mom wouldn't look at me the same. Then suddenly, without explanation, she yanked my purse from my shoulder and dumped everything onto the floor. She picked up a crumpled piece of foil like it was evidence in a trial.

My breath caught. I stared, confused. I didn't recognize it. Didn't understand what she thought she'd found.

But then it hit me. The foil wasn't from the trip. It had been in my purse before I even left. My mother hadn't planted it for a smuggling run—she had been using my bag as a hiding place. And now, coming down from her high and needing a fix, she went looking for it.

Only it wasn't there.

And somehow, that was my fault.

That's when I realized she hadn't just let me into her life—she had folded me into her addiction. I had become part of her cycle without even knowing it.

Still, I said nothing. Not because I didn't want to speak, but because I had been taught: mothers are untouchable. You protect them, even from themselves. You stay quiet.

When I found the spoon later, the one with the burn marks, the one that confirmed everything—I didn't rage. I didn't yell. I just grieved.

Because the woman who was supposed to protect me had used me.

Because I realized I was becoming her.

I felt numb. Hopeless. Unmotivated. I wasn't looking for ways to move forward—I was just trying to survive. My days became a fog. Even a word as small as "shut up" could send me into tears. I didn't recognize myself.

But then, slowly, I started clawing my way back. Gospel music. Sermons on TV. I got a physical. I went to the dentist. I started taking care of myself piece by piece, from the inside out.

Because if I didn't, I knew where I'd end up.

I watched my mother cry when my brother got arrested—not out of grief, but because it gave her access to his things. I saw what joy looked like in disguise. I saw what envy could do.

And I said, "Not me."

I wouldn't stay in a place where no one wanted better.

"Running to what I was running from"—that's what this chapter is about.

I thought I was seeking love. Belonging. But I was really chasing the exact life I was trying to escape. I'd spent years trying to prove I wasn't her, only to step into her world like it was mine.

I didn't know.

But now I do.

Because when I looked in the mirror, I didn't just see myself—I saw her. And all I heard was Auntie Gina's voice echoing in my ear: "You're going to end up just like your mother."

And for the first time, I wasn't afraid she might be right.

I was afraid she already was.

But what I didn't know—what I couldn't see through the fog of pills and pain and broken promises—was that sometimes you have to fall all the way to the bottom before you remember you have wings.

And I was about to hit ground so hard it would either kill me or wake me up.

The choice was mine.

And I was running out of time to make it.

CHAPTER 6
The Beating That Broke the Illusion

Sometimes the very cocoon you thought would protect you becomes the thing that nearly destroys you.

The day I was moving out started beautiful—warm, hopeful. My new apartment was almost like a townhouse they were building in the neighborhood. Fresh start energy surrounded me.

I'd been setting boundaries with my mom, telling her no more and more. Working longer hours, pulling away. The more I did that, the angrier she got. With my brother gone, it was just me and her, and the money she'd been depending on from him for drugs now needed to come from me.

My friend came to help move my stuff—mattress, clothes, little knick-knacks. As I moved everything out, my mom stood there getting angrier and angrier. Her eyes, her face—building up rage like a storm gathering strength.

"I'm just going around the corner," I told her. "I'm still here. Whatever you need, if I got it, I got you."

For the last hour of moving, she disappeared. I figured she was emotional, hiding in her room. I didn't want to bother her.

As I went to the bathroom to get the last thing—a three-drawer plastic organizer—I heard noise behind me. I turned around as my mom drew back her fist and punched me dead in my face.

I fell into the tub, pulling down the shower curtain. Pure confusion. Pure shock.

Next thing I knew, she had a brick in her other hand—from the snake tank with the python they kept. She threw that brick at me, then started stomping. Punching my face, my side, my feet.

"You stealing from me! You taking everything from me! You think I'm stupid!"

"Mom, no, these are my things that I bought. I'm not going anywhere far."

I couldn't fight back. The way I was raised—you don't put your hands on your parents. My natural reaction was flight, not fight. Curl up or run away.

This went on for ten minutes. Everyone was loading the truck, so it was just her and me in the house.

Finally, her boyfriend heard the commotion and pulled her off. "What is going on?"

"She stealing from me!"

I climbed out of the tub—blood dripping from my nose,

crying, snot running down, bruised, barely able to walk. I ran outside.

My friend immediately called the police. "Oh, hell no."

When the police came, they looked at me, then at her. She claimed I hit her first, but they said, "No, ma'am. Look at her and look at you."

They handcuffed her. "She already got a warrant out for her arrest, so she gotta go."

I'm like, *what the hell?* Rule number one in the hood—you don't call the police. You definitely don't call the police on your mama.

They took her away. I went to my new apartment, bandaged myself up, trying to process what had just happened.

Then the phone rang. I thought maybe it was my mom, that she'd calmed down.

It was my brother Marquis from jail. "Hey, what the f*ck? Sis, you got mom locked up!"

"I didn't even call—" I tried to explain.

"I'm sorry. She's going through withdrawal. She ain't getting that dope."

That was the final realization. She had gone from weed to cocaine to pills to crack to fentanyl. Everything clicked into place like a complete circle.

She did four days, then came to my apartment when she got out. "This is mine right here." Breaking up with her boyfriend because he "shouldn't have let the police take me away," she brought a new boyfriend—my exact same age, twenty-one, but looking forty from drugs.

Within days, I caught them sniffing together in my living room. *I gotta get out of here.*

I went drinking with friends, got drunk, threw up before

driving. Ended up driving on the opposite side of traffic—literally driving toward headlights. DUI, weed charges, two days in the drunk tank.

When I got out, my mother was nowhere to be found. I'd lost my job for missing days with no call, no show.

No job, new apartment, DUI and weed charges, dealing with my mom situation.

I needed weed—not learning from what just happened.

When my mom came around that evening and I told her what happened, she lost it again. "You being so stupid! What's wrong with you!"

The neighbor came out telling her to calm down. Next thing I know, they're arguing, and I'm defending my mother. We all ended up fussing. The police charged me with verbal assault on an officer—didn't even know that was a thing—and trespassing because the apartment complex said I had to go for causing too much commotion.

Back in my car. Car got repossessed. Lost my apartment. Three or four charges against me. Back staying with my mom in motels she was turning into apartments.

Everything I had was falling apart.

Court dates kept coming. Every time I tried to pick myself up, I got pulled back down.

One particular court date was devastating. My dad was there—not hiding, but present like he knew about the case. The paperwork must have gone to his house since I didn't have an address.

I was so embarrassed that he now knew where I was and what was going on in my life. I hadn't talked to him in two years. I acted like I didn't see him because I was ashamed, but in the back of my mind, I was hoping he would reach out.

I got into programs—ASAP for the DUI, counseling classes, drug tests. God was stepping in, forcing me to clean myself up.

For the weed charge, they told me I had to serve two days in jail. I'd never done jail time before.

When I checked myself in, they made me take my braids out, remove all jewelry, anything I could hurt myself with. Squat and cough, get naked. People yelling, everything stinking, officers looking down on you like you're nothing.

Cement cell, blue mattress, sink, toilet, camera watching the whole time. No blanket, no pillow. Cold bologna sandwiches I couldn't eat.

I cried myself to sleep that first night. The worst part was trying to wash with clothes on because of that camera. Standing at the sink with wet clothes, cold, no blanket, miserable.

"Only one more day. Just one more day."

When I finally got released, I called my grandmother. "I am never going back to jail. I could barely do two days."

My grandmother told me the relationship with my mom was completely ruptured. "You got to go to court again."

"For what? I just did jail time."

"That beating she gave you when you were moving out."

I went to court standing against my mom. She was high with dark blue hair, lying through her teeth. "I raised this girl since she was a baby. I didn't beat her that bad. This was a regular beating."

The judge had her paperwork. The reason she got taken away in the first place was because she had a warrant for back child support she hadn't given to my father.

He looked at her like, "How were you raising her and owing child support at the same time?"

Her ex-boyfriend testified about the brick and everything.

The judge told her she had to do a week in jail and gave her a restraining order—she couldn't come around me for five years.

I'm standing there like, *what in the world is going on?* I didn't ask for this to happen.

My grandmother said, "Come stay with me. We're gonna work on getting your life back together."

Church—Sunday service and Bible study. If you were living in her house, you were going to both. "We're gonna get you a job, fix your credit, show you how to pay bills. You're gonna be paying me. We're gonna get you on food stamps."

I got a temp job at UPS as a customer service agent. My grandmother would take me back and forth to work. I was able to pay court fees, fines, DUI fees—thousands of dollars. Got my car back.

Throughout all of this, I still hadn't had a conversation with my father. We still weren't on those terms. My grandmother kept us updated about each other, but no direct communication.

We ended up seeing each other at my grandmother's cookout. We spoke, but the relationship was weird. Like seeing a cousin. No father-daughter love at all.

The person I was closest to, I didn't even know anymore.

When problems started between my father and grandmother—her speaking negatively about him—what was once rescue and peace became gossiping. I wasn't comfortable.

I began staying at friends' houses, somewhere away from her. When I felt that happening, I was like, no. We're not going backwards.

God had separated me from everything I knew and didn't know. My dad and I were strangers. My mom and I were strangers with a restraining order. My little brother was locked up. Now my grandmother was talking about the one person I couldn't agree with her about.

I was back to being alone. *What in the world is happening? What do I do?*

I went to church one Sunday when my grandmother was out of town. During the altar call—not for salvation, but for backsliding—I went up and told the truth.

"I just want deliverance from marijuana and pills. I want complete deliverance because I feel like I just gotta get this away from me."

Four people laid hands on me in a circle, prayed, rebuked, and cast out the spirit of addiction from my body.

From that day to this day, I still cannot smoke marijuana. Even if I tried a hit, it makes me so paranoid, so delusional, so stupid that I can't function. It literally took the taste out of my mouth.

That was my first real, genuine face-to-face connection and miracle experience with God doing miraculous things in me that I couldn't do for myself.

That was the beginning of understanding that it doesn't matter—it's not my mom, not my dad, not my grandmother, not my brother. Nobody can do for me what God can do. I cannot put my trust in man because they are just humans, just as I am.

> *Just when I thought I'd lost everything—my mother, my father, my freedom, my home—I discovered that sometimes you have to be stripped down to nothing to find everything you've been searching for.*

CHAPTER 7
Wings in the Waiting

There's a season when a butterfly must learn to trust her wings before she can truly fly. The most beautiful flight often comes after the longest wait.

I had begun to form a real foundation with God again.

Going to church on my own, taking notes, referencing and reading back through them—this changed everything for me. I got a friend at work who was on the same page when it came to relationship with God. She became one of my closest friends, someone who'd been through the mud herself and made it out.

Some Fridays after work, we'd go to our favorite Mexican restaurant and discuss life over nachos.

"Don't you think it's time for you to start dating?" she'd ask.

"No, I don't think so. I want to focus on myself right now. I'm trying to build my life again."

I got offered a full-time position at the job where I'd been temping. Three promotions while still temporary, then finally permanent as an international rep. God was protecting and blessing me.

I started creating daily devotional emails to my friend—taking my notes from church and making motivational messages. She loved hearing what I'd learned from sermons, and slowly more people were added to that daily word. When I'd miss a day, they'd ask, "Where's the word today?"

But I was still embarrassed about my past. I didn't feel comfortable with people looking to me for wisdom because I'm no Jesus—I'm just human trying to figure it out.

My relationship with my dad was getting better too. We began having actual conversations. You could tell there was still some strife, but I felt comfortable enough to communicate because I was starting to do better.

I'd also gone back to school at Regent University, a Christian-based school, to get my bachelor's degree in psychology. That was keeping my focus sharp.

After my friend's persistent suggestions about dating, I went on a leap to at least see what was out there. But I'd stopped my birth control—couldn't afford the doctor visits.

I ended up getting pregnant, and I was devastated. Absolutely devastated.

Finally, I had gotten so far, come so far, and now I was literally falling into the box where everybody said I was going to be—just like her.

I made the decision to abort my baby. That was hard. Really, really hard.

The guilt I felt when you've tried to build and maintain your faith in God, and you're about to commit what feels like murder. On top of that, knowing the family and what everybody said about how you were going to be just like her—all of that played back.

I was broken again.

The day I went to the facility to terminate, protesters stood in front chanting, "Murderer! Baby killer! Why don't you just have it and give it away?"

It was horrible. I cried and kept walking.

I took the medication and went into deep depression. Begging God for forgiveness. I felt like either way I messed up—if I had the baby, if I didn't have the baby, it was a mess up.

I didn't forgive myself for years. Probably not until I was thirty-four or thirty-five did I finally accept God's forgiveness and forgive myself, understanding that God would have made a way had I chosen to continue with that pregnancy.

I didn't tell many people. I did tell my father, and he wasn't proud. It put another rift in our relationship that we were trying to rebuild.

I distanced myself from everything and went into a shell, trying to hold onto what I believed God was watching over me for.

During this time, something came upon me: "Start looking at houses. Maybe you guys can move."

I'd just started the new job, but I followed the word. I got into programs with Southside Communities Development and Housing Opportunities Made Equal. They helped clean up my credit completely—I needed a 620 score, and mine was in the 500s from the car repossession.

I worked to save money, pay off debt, and stay spiritually grounded. God was my only dependence to survive.

I finished the classes, got certificates. The programs helped with down payments and finding or building your first home.

At this point, I decided to try the relationship thing again. I met this older guy—three years younger than my father—still in that mindset wanting a father figure.

I moved out of my grandmother's house and moved in with him. The day before, I was sitting in my car looking at the sky, bawling my eyes out. I knew in my heart I wasn't supposed to move in with him, but I wanted to so bad.

As I looked at the sky crying, the clouds began to form two shapes—one like a "Y" and the other like a house. In my mind, I thought that was God telling me yes. I took that as confirmation.

It was the worst decision I could have made.

I stopped going to church as often. I had no clue the severity of mind games and heartbreak that relationship would bring. He didn't have a job—he was a drug dealer. He didn't take care of his kids. He was depending on other women to survive.

I kept asking him to come to church with me. He wouldn't, but I kept praying for him. I asked him to try to get his youngest daughter every other weekend, find him a construction job so we could become better together.

For a while, it seemed like he was trying. He got a job, things were going better. I adopted a little Yorkie named Gucci. We had our own little family.

Then he lost the job.

I ended up working extra hours, getting promotions, finding my niche in human resources. I began to spoil him, spending thousands, giving him half my check, trying to keep him happy.

But the signs were there. Female deodorants in the house. My lotion halfway gone. A bundle of weave missing after Christmas.

The neighbor mentioned seeing a girl going into the house.

Bitter, Oppressed, or Blessed

When I asked, he said it was just his cousin Renita. I knew her—we'd hung out, gone shopping, gone clubbing.

One night, I checked his phone and found text messages between him and this "cousin" saying good night like lovers. That was the final straw.

I called everyone—his mom, his brother—asking who this person really was. They all said, "That's our cousin."

My friend suggested, "Let's drive by the house during lunch."

We drove by, and her car was there. We went in the house, and they were having sex on our bed.

My heart was broken. This man had tricked me for three or four years that this girl was his cousin when she was really his side piece. All the money I'd been spending was going towards them.

The next day, my friend, the neighbor, and I packed up all my stuff and my dog. Just as I was putting the last thing in my car, he pulled up.

"What's going on? What you doing?"

"I'm leaving you. I already know about you and Renita."

"Oh, okay. Bye."

The shock on all our faces—he didn't even try to fight for the relationship.

I returned to my grandmother's house, but this time I was ready. I had already gotten the certificates for building a house. They had new properties, and I signed up.

Within a year, I'd be able to move into my own place.

The first couple months after I left him, he started doing drive-bys at seven in the morning. "I miss you." Once the money ran out, he was coming around. He was stalking me at my job too.

My friend downloaded a dating app on my phone. "You don't have to go on dates. You can just scroll through pictures."

The app sat on my phone. I might swipe a picture or two, but that was it.

I was getting promotions at work, making more money, meeting with people to begin the process of breaking ground on my house. We broke ground and built the foundation. I picked a three-bedroom, three-bath house in Southside—my first home. I was so proud of myself.

My ex was still stalking to the point where I had to tell my job. He drove beside me as I was walking into work, calling me names, making threats.

My job let me park in the garage unless I got a restraining order. But then he began accessing my email somehow, knowing when I was on the dating app, knowing where I was shopping.

I immediately changed all passwords, ordered new cards, went to the courthouse and requested a restraining order to be effective immediately.

The guy from the dating app had reached back out, but I kind of ignored him because I was living in fear from my ex.

My friend told me to check the app again. "Did that guy ever respond back?"

So I did.

We had a typical online conversation. "Hi, I really liked your pictures. My name is Butterfly. What's yours?"

"Hey, I'm Lion. I liked your pictures too. What do you like to do?"

When he said he took care of his mom who had a brain aneurysm from being on drugs, and I told him I had to be raised by my dad because my mom's also on drugs, we both looked at each other through the screen like, *whoa.*

Two broken people from broken homes, both scarred by addiction, both raised without their mothers—what were the odds?

Bitter, Oppressed, or Blessed

Sometimes God puts you exactly where you need to be, with exactly who you need to meet, right when you're finally ready to fly.

CHAPTER 8
The Lion and the Butterfly

When a butterfly meets a lion, the world says it's impossible. But sometimes the most unlikely combinations create the most extraordinary love stories.

We had been talking online for about a month when he asked if I wanted to meet in person. Because of what I was dealing with—the restraining order, constantly looking over my shoulder—I was terrified.

My friends and I were going to a Jamaican festival in Virginia Beach, then to the after-party at a club off Jefferson Davis Highway.

"I'll ask him if he'll meet me there. At least it'll be a group of us."

When I called him, he was like, "Yeah, I'm up for that."

We ended up meeting at the after-party, but it was dead—nobody was in there.

"Y'all, we can go. This is wack."

"Ain't you supposed to be meeting somebody?"

"Yeah, but I really don't want to. We can just go."

"No, Sierra, you can't be scared of guys all your life."

I texted him: "Hey, Lion, this is Butterfly. We're here if you want to meet up still."

"Yeah, I'm already out. I was ready to head to this other club, but I'll come back there."

"You really don't have to because it's pretty dead."

"That's fine. I'm pulling up. I'll be there."

When I saw Lion walking in—blue kangol hat, white polo with blue logo, dark blue Levi jeans, fresh Jordans, goatee perfectly lined—I was like, *oh wow, he looks even better in person.*

He noticed me at the bar and came up. "Butterfly?"

"Yeah, but you can just call me Butter. All my friends call me Butter."

"Okay, Butter. I like that. I'm Lion. You're beautiful in person. You look really good."

We talked for so long that we shut the restaurant down. They had to tell us they were closing. Neither of us had noticed it was getting empty.

He paid the check like a gentleman, walked me out, told me he really enjoyed himself, and gave me a hug.

That was the beginning of our love story.

From there, we talked on the phone every day. Every weekend we'd go on dates—Dave & Busters, cookouts. About a month in, he introduced me to his children and his mother.

I remembered something my grandmother told me: "If you ever meet a guy and see how he takes care of his mother, that's how he's gonna take care of you. And if you see how he treats his kids, that's how he's gonna treat your kids."

Watching him with them, I fell deeper in love.

When I had to tell him about my restraining order, he went into protective mode instantly. "What? Nah, I ain't going nowhere. Pack your stuff. Move out of your grandmother's house. You're gonna move in with me, and I'm going to court with you."

"Hold on, slow down. We haven't even been intimate yet."

"Alright, fine. If you don't want to do that yet, I'm gonna be driving behind you, and I won't go in the court building, but I'll wait outside."

That Monday was my court date. The judge granted me the extension—two years. My ex was there, just staring. I tried not to make eye contact.

When I left, I got a call from Lion while I was in the car. "Look, go slow. I'm gonna tell you how to turn. That dude parked behind your car so he could follow you."

"But the judge literally just told him to stay away from me."

"Yeah, all right, we'll see. Bust a right right here. Now bust a left. When you get to the end of the street, it's gonna be a cul-de-sac. Make a U-turn. He's gonna see you coming out, but he's not gonna see me, so he's gonna go a different way. I'm gonna follow him, and you go the opposite way."

I did exactly what he said. Lion followed my ex to a McDonald's parking lot and just watched him, camping out to see what his next move was.

Lion called me: "Did you make it home safe?"

"Yeah."

"I'm not taking back my request. You got a couple months to think about it, but I definitely think you should move in with me."

After the court case, Lion began picking me up and taking me to work, or having one of his friends do it. He was constantly making sure I was safe.

When my birthday came in May, he took me to DC for a friend's restaurant opening. He bought Dom Pérignon, took me to the mall to get my outfit, really showed me a good time. I met some of his friends from DC.

We still hadn't been intimate yet.

June came and we were scheduled to go to Miami. I was nervous—this was another state entirely. But I trusted him.

I knew that weekend was probably going to be the weekend, but I'd made it clear: if we become intimate, we're together. We're boyfriend and girlfriend.

"Okay, that's cool. That means you're moving in."

Miami was like the signing agreement. We took pictures everywhere. He enjoyed his first plane ride. I felt special being the first person to get him on a plane—most of his friends were shocked because they could never get him on one.

One night, after dinner and drinks, we made it official. We became intimate.

Miami was signed, sealed, and delivered.

I moved in with him, and things were great. He's older—about seven years apart—but he was completely different from anyone I'd ever met. He didn't want anything from me. He always poured into me. Everybody respected him. He was this king protector.

It was time for him to meet my father. I was ready but nervous because my dad and I still hadn't had that full conversation. We were getting closer, but it wasn't the relationship we used to have.

We'd been dating and living together about six months when my dad's birthday came in January. My stepmother planned a birthday dinner, and I brought Lion.

He gave my father a bottle of Moët as a birthday present. My dad seemed like, "Okay, cool, he seems like a decent guy."

My dad had already done his research. He told me he'd heard from the streets that Lion was solid—"He'll give you the shirt off his back. You made a good choice."

My house was finally finished right before my birthday. I asked Lion, "Are you gonna move with me? This is going to be your house too."

"Yeah, of course. We can rent out my house for income."

We moved into the house I'd built together. We were happy, content, traveling everywhere—Miami, California riding ATVs in the mountains, Jamaica, Vegas, New York.

We'd been together officially for about two and a half years when my birthday came around again. Lion had already, unbeknownst to me, talked to my dad and asked for my hand in marriage.

He planned to take me to Arlington, Virginia, with another couple. We ended up at this steakhouse, and I was starving from being on the road all day. Lion was acting weird—nervous, going to the bathroom and staying forever.

As I'm sitting there looking for him, his friend puts a wedding cake topper on the table—a bride and groom figurine. I'm confused, looking at them like, "What's going on?"

Their eyes kept darting to the figurine, then to me, then to the side. I turned to my right, and there was Lion on one knee with a ring.

"Will you marry me?"

I started crying and bawling. "Yes, yes, yes! Of course!"

The whole restaurant started cheering and clapping. Other couples sent over champagne, stopping by to give advice. Everyone wanted to take our pictures.

When Lion went to the bathroom earlier, he'd put on a white blazer over his white tee. That explained all the crazy stops we'd made—he'd brought the blazer for the proposal.

I called my dad, and he was happy and excited. "Congratulations." He already knew, of course.

Lion said, "You know, I appreciate you. You're a vast contradiction from other women. Not only did you accept me and everything I came with, but you helped me take care of my mom. I had prayed for God to send me my wife, and that was you."

We had a beautiful wedding with red, black, and white colors at an art gallery in Petersburg. Four bridesmaids, a ring bearer, photographers, all the food, DJ—everything.

My stepmom planned the whole thing and my dad paid for the venue. It was like, "You're finally doing what I knew you were capable of doing, and I'm proud of you."

That's when my dad and I had the full conversation that changed everything.

He said he was proud, but I had just messed up so much. Then he did something that transformed our relationship—he apologized for telling me I couldn't come home at nineteen.

"I wish I could have done it differently. The anger was because you came to me high and entitled. I wish I could have handled it differently."

That moment changed my whole mindframe. I had nothing but forgiveness because I had to take responsibility for my part. I had hurt him. Me coming to him in that state reminded him of everything he'd given up his life to prevent, and I was choosing to become that person.

Him apologizing made me see him as human. I finally saw a man, not this king that doesn't make mistakes. My dad was human, regular, going to make mistakes. He's not a superhero.

It was like a weight lifted off my shoulders. Him being able to apologize and show his humanity opened my eyes to also apologize for all the disappointments I'd put him through.

Even though we couldn't rewrite history, we could both get past it and grow into the new people we were becoming. We could get that father-daughter relationship back.

We had to pick a pastor for the wedding. The realtor assigned to me from the housing program was T. Turner—Sylvester Turner. My grandmother mentioned he was also a pastor, so I reached out.

He agreed but said we needed counseling sessions because he knew me but didn't know Lion.

The day we went to meet Pastor Turner at Pilgrim Baptist Church in Woolfin Court, something amazing happened. Lion was nervous about the area—if you're from Richmond, you know Fairfield and Woolfin Court aren't exactly friendly neighbors.

As we walked in, the pastor was waiting. When he saw Lion, his face lit up.

"What?!"

"T! Mr. T!"

"Ronnie! Lion!"

They hugged, reminiscing. The pastor said, "I was wondering what happened to you. You were one of my favorite students. I always wondered if you were okay."

Lion turned to me: "This is my mentor I told you about, who kept me in line, trying to keep me out of the streets."

Pastor Turner said, "He was the president of the community group I was running. I always wondered what happened to him."

The pastor looked at both of us and smiled: "Your name's alone, Butterfly. How did you tame a Lion?"

We both laughed because that was the running joke between Chesterfield and Fairfield—how did this even work out?

We did our counseling sessions, and everything went well. It took us about a year and six months to plan the wedding.

But as we got closer to the date, the devil tried everything to stop us. My ex popped up again after five years. A pipe burst in our upstairs bathroom, flooding our entire house. Two months before the wedding, Lion was in a motorcycle accident with a Honda mini truck. The lady rolled over him twice. He ended up in ICU for three days with fractures and burn marks.

He could barely walk and was in a wheelchair. I'm trying to take care of him, his disabled mother, our flooded house, and plan a wedding.

"We're doing this wedding," he said. "We spent this money, invited people—we're doing it."

The devil did not want this marriage. We had so many trials before that day, but we made it.

It was a great day. We had so much food that my dad ended up making to-go boxes for the homeless in the area. We left in a limo, went home, changed, and got ready for our honeymoon to Jamaica.

Two broken souls had found wholeness in each other. A butterfly had learned to dance with a lion. But marriage is just the beginning of the story, and the biggest test of our love—and our faith—was still ahead.

CHAPTER 9
Delayed but Not Denied

Sometimes the greatest blessings come disguised as the longest waits. What feels like denial is actually divine timing.

Since our wedding day—September 19, 2019—we had been trying to get pregnant.

I was thirty-three, and we were ready to expand our family. Then COVID hit in 2020, and everyone's world changed. For us, thank God, COVID was actually peaceful. It was literally the honeymoon phase because all we had was each other. While many couples got sick of each other, we got closer.

We weren't focused on getting pregnant because of everything going on—babies in hospitals, both parents couldn't be there for delivery. Too many mixed feelings about being pregnant during that time.

2021 came, my husband was doing better, the house had been cleaned up from the flood. We were doing good.

Then in February, my husband's mother passed.

I was downstairs in the living room drinking wine with a friend when I went to check on her. Her eyes just didn't look normal—kind of rolled up.

"May? Miss May?" She didn't respond.

I moved her arm and it dropped. My heart dropped at the same time.

The ambulance came, tried to resuscitate her three times. By the time Lion got home, they were saying she was gone.

My husband was screaming and crying, going to her body, hugging her. I'm crouched down crying and yelling.

I felt guilty because we lost her on my watch, but thank God he didn't blame me.

Technically, she wasn't supposed to survive as long as she had—twelve or thirteen years since her brain aneurysm. What I believe is that she felt safe in our home. She felt okay with her son being in good hands. She made it to his wedding day, and now she was ready to go.

Lion began to change after that. It was mixed feelings of loss but also freedom. For twelve or thirteen years, he'd never been fully free. Now he was, but his anchor was gone.

He began to go out. One day became two days, became three, four, five days. He was just out all the time. Instead of coming together, it became competition.

"Well, if you're going out with friends, you need to have friends too." So it became less of us going out together and more of us competing with each other.

The competition escalated. Instead of being home by twelve, he'd come in at one. "Okay, well if you can come in at one, I'm gonna come in at two." Then he's coming in at three. The ultimate was when I came in at four in the morning.

That was the nail that broke the camel's back.

We made an agreement to be in the house by 3:30 AM if we were going out.

I stopped competing and focused on maybe having a kid since we had the extra room now.

We'd been trying for three years at this point. "We need to go get looked at."

Everything was fine with my body. His sperm count was beyond fine—they said normal was five million, and he had 150 million.

They suggested IUI—a process where they monitor the female's cycle and when you ovulate, they insert the sperm to ensure perfect timing.

We tried it the first time in 2021—it didn't work. We tried again at the beginning of 2022—it didn't work.

We were crushed. We'd taken at least twenty pregnancy tests, and it just wasn't working. We'd just lost his mom. It was way too much.

We had a miscarriage—an ectopic pregnancy where the egg attached to the outer wall. I'm blaming myself, thinking this was because I didn't bring forth the child I was supposed to long ago.

I felt like Lion was thinking he'd gotten catfished—married a woman who can't even give him kids.

The fighting between us began. Literally every two weeks we were arguing about something small, constantly at each other's throats.

In February 2022, Lion and I had gotten into an argument, and he left the house. A week later, something about that day didn't feel right.

I decided to check his phone while he was in the shower. There was a 757 number. Reading the messages: "Okay babe, I'll be waiting." Lion replied, "I'm coming now." Then "I'm here, I'm outside." The response: "Come on up."

My heart was crushed. Completely and utterly broken.

I ran into the bathroom while he was in the shower, screaming, "What the f*ck is this? Are you cheating?"

"What are you talking about? You bugging out."

I showed him the messages. His head dropped. No more denying—it was right in his face.

"I'm sorry."

I broke down, ran to put on clothes to leave. Lion jumped out of the shower, chasing me, begging. "Please don't go. I'm sorry. I didn't mean for you to see that. I thought I deleted it."

"I can't believe you did this to me. You knew what I came out of with my past relationship. I only had two rules—don't cheat on me and don't put your hands on me."

Two weeks later, his phone rang while we were in the car. He hit decline and said he needed to go back to the house. Something told me to follow him.

I crept up behind him, and he was on the phone with this female. I went from broken and depressed to rage. Absolute rage.

I slammed the door open. "What are you doing?"

"I was trying to tell her don't ever call my phone again."

"Give me your phone!" I called the number back. "Are you calling my husband? You just saw him last Wednesday."

"I don't know what you're talking about."

I blocked her and told him, "You gotta go. You need to leave."

The next week, he came back wanting to talk. "We'll go to counseling. I'll do whatever you want."

A couple days later: "I've been thinking about counseling, and I really don't know if I want to do that."

I checked his phone again and saw he was reaching out to females on Instagram, sending his wedding picture and saying, "Yeah, I just got married." I saw texts with his friends about going to strip clubs—his friends calling it his "second home."

With the pressure of being caught, the tame lion turned into rage. He grabbed me by my throat and slammed me on the couch.

I lost it—kicking, punching, swinging, yelling, "Get out! Get out!"

It was pouring rain outside. I opened the door and started throwing his clothes outside in the rain.

"Fine, I'm leaving!"

Both of us were bruised from the altercation. After I kicked him out, I called my dad: "Come change the locks. He's gotta go. We're done. He put his hands on me. He cheated on me. I'm divorcing."

But then came the moment that changed everything.

May 2023. My birthday. He took me to my first live boxing match—Gervonta Davis versus Ryan Garcia in New York at the Barclays Center. He took me to the Versace store, got my outfit, trying to show me whatever he had to prove he loved me.

I'm smiling on the outside, but inside I'm like, "I'm so tired of all this."

At the end of the boxing match, just as we were five feet from the exit doors, shots rang out outside. The entire crowd from outside began pouring back into the building. It was a complete stampede.

I froze. People were running through glass windows, breaking them, getting trampled.

Instantly, Lion wrapped his arms around me. It was like I was floating. He used his body as a shield from the stampede and gunfire, guiding me to a pillar away from the door. He hid both of us behind the pillar.

As people continued to run past, he dropped down and picked up someone who'd fallen, telling them to hold onto his shoulders and stand behind him.

After the shock wore off, I realized why God had placed us together. He had just risked his life and was willing to give his life for me. He literally used his body as a shield with no idea what was coming—people, stampede, glass, gunfire. He was willing to take it all but made sure he shielded and protected me.

That day, one of the walls I'd put up from his mistakes came down. I could offer forgiveness because he was willing to give his life for mine.

We're still going through counseling, but I still wasn't fully okay. I still had trust issues, was still going through his phone, still bringing up the adultery.

November came. We went to my family's house for Thanksgiving, ate, had drinks like normal. I'd been feeling weird, but I'd completely given up the thought of having a child. We'd been trying since 2019—here it is 2023. I just gave it to God.

I went home around eleven, tired and sleepy. Lion was like, "I'm gonna go out with my dad to this older bar."

As I'm looking in the cabinet for toilet paper, I saw a pregnancy test. "I thought I threw all these away. It's eleven o'clock at night. I'm about to pee. Let me just pee on this and throw it away so it won't be a complete waste."

I peed on it, set it down, went to the room. Five minutes later, curiosity got me. I went back to look.

It said pregnant.

Instantly I'm bawling. I drop to my knees. "This is impossible. What?"

All I hear and feel is God saying, "You wanted a reason to stay. You wanted me to tell you this is ordained by me, and this is your soulmate. Here you go. You have to stay. Get those thoughts out of your head. You're not going anywhere."

I called Lion and FaceTimed him, showing him the pregnancy test.

"You have to come home."

He got there in five minutes flat. He grabbed the test, hugged me, and we both started crying, dropping to the floor on our knees, crying and shocked that this was happening.

We'd been trying since 2019—here it is 2023 at eleven o'clock at night, and we see that we're pregnant.

That moment changed everything. I realized we were no longer forgotten by God. After we'd stopped trying so hard and surrendered to God, and Lion had surrendered his life for mine, and I'd begun to forgive half of what he'd done—it was like God saying, "Okay, y'all are ready for this blessing. I can trust you with having this baby."

Instantly, the tamed lion I knew was back.

> *Sometimes the greatest blessings come not when we're demanding them, but when we're finally ready to receive them. Delayed but not denied—that's the story of God's perfect timing.*

CHAPTER 10
Full Circle Faith

Sometimes the greatest miracle isn't just the butterfly emerging from the cocoon—it's realizing that everything that tried to break you was actually building you.

The day I went in for a routine checkup became the day I would meet my miracle.

"Miss Briley, we're gonna have to check you in. We think you're gonna have to have this baby now."

"What? I'm five weeks early. I don't understand."

They told me he had stopped growing. He hadn't grown in two weeks, and we had to get him out now.

Literally, the day I go in for a doctor's appointment, they tell me I'm giving birth. I immediately called Lion, my dad, family. "They're gonna induce me. This is what's happening."

I was excited but scared. This was five weeks early.

I'm doing videos to my son like, "Hey, this is what's going on. You're coming early. You said you wanted to get out. You were tired of mommy's food. You wanted to see the world yourself."

As I sat up to let them do the epidural, the godmother was holding me up, and my water broke on her.

"What the hell is this?"

"Don't move!" the doctor said.

That was pretty funny. They successfully got the epidural, and I literally set a timer on my phone to push the button every ten to fifteen minutes.

This was the 24th—that evening. That date was crazy because that's also Lion's daughter's birthday. She was turning fifteen that day.

Lion was like, "Do you mind if I go to her dinner real quick?"

"Okay, whatever. Do what you want to do."

My parents were like, "Why did you tell him it was okay for him to leave? You're literally about to give birth to his child."

I knew Lion didn't do well with hospitals. The hospital represented nothing positive for him growing up.

As he left, I began to have contractions. His uncle stayed with me because he used to be in the army and deliver babies. My dad and stepmom would switch out shifts.

The 25th came. I still hadn't had the baby, but I was starting to dilate more. Before I got to eight centimeters, Lion wasn't there when suddenly it was like a bomb of nurses and doctors came running into the room.

"Your blood pressure—the baby's blood pressure is above

200. We have to get you calmed down. We have to get the baby calmed down."

It was like the boxing match moment. I froze. I heard what was going on, but I didn't hear what was going on.

"Get up on your knees in a crawling position. We need to get this blood pressure down, get your heart rate down, get the baby's heart rate down."

I just blacked out. Unbeknownst to me, my son and I were about to die, and my husband wasn't there.

After they finally got both our blood pressures down to a stable point, they wanted to deliver immediately. I was only eight centimeters, and Lion wasn't there.

"No, you know, I'm not ready yet."

The doctor was like, "I can do it. We don't have to wait on your doctor."

"No." I was really close and connected to my OBGYN. He'd delivered triplets, had over thirty years of experience. "Especially nowadays, Black women don't often make it out of the hospital with their kids, and he's coming premature. I'm gonna wait for him."

They called him at five in the morning. He said, "She's only eight centimeters. She can go fully to ten. We're not gonna force her and the baby when they have the ability to get to where they need to be. This is how we end up forcing and killing Black women. We're not going to do this."

I called Lion: "I need you to be present. Come around."

Finally, I hit ten centimeters. The doctor comes in: "All right, we're ready. You're about to push."

Lion's not in the room. My parents are like, "Forget this. We'll cut the cord."

"No." I called Lion: "Come in here right now. I'm about to deliver right now."

He comes in, and my parents leave because they're completely pissed at him.

I'm bawling crying. "Lion, I had a birth plan set up, and I want my dad and stepmom in here with all three of y'all. I don't know what y'all have going on, but it's not time. Get over it. Y'all get along for just this moment while I'm having this baby."

I told him to go get my parents. They came in. Lion was holding one leg, my stepmother was holding the other, and my dad was up above making sure I stayed cool.

I told them I wanted gospel music playing as my son came into the world.

In the middle of me pushing, my stepmom was able to record the entire moment of my son coming into the world.

Once he made it out, my dad was ecstatic, grabbing me and kissing my head. My husband had this big smile on his face. The doctor handed him the scissors to cut the cord.

I'm exhausted, and they take him away to clean him up. My mind went to, "Why haven't I heard him cry? It's silent. Why haven't I heard him cry?"

My dad's like, "Calm down. I see his eyes. He's opening his eyes. He's okay."

"But I don't hear him. Why can't I hear him?"

They bring him to me wrapped up for maybe not even a minute—long enough to take a picture—then they took him away.

"What's going on? What's wrong?"

"No, he's fine. You gotta remember, he's premature. He came at only three pounds, six ounces. We gotta get you together."

We named him Eziah Divine Briley—God's gift, God's divine gift.

Bitter, Oppressed, or Blessed

Eziah had to go to the NICU because of how small he was. Lion went to be with him, and my parents ended up leaving because Lion had disappeared during the delivery and came back empty-handed. No balloons, no teddy bear, no "thank you for having my baby"—nothing.

My parents had enough. "The selfishness is beyond."

Once they left, Lion became present and stayed in the room with me the whole time. He was going back and forth checking on Eziah because for twenty-four hours, I wasn't allowed to see him.

After twenty-four hours, I was able to go see my baby. He had all these tubes, but he was moving his little arms and looked like he was trying to talk. He was inside this little tank with tubes taped to him, little alien look with black eyes.

I just fell in love. I was in complete bliss.

I stayed in the hospital for about a week because they were monitoring my blood pressure. Every chance I got, I was down at the NICU. They were amazed because I wasn't bleeding like normal. "You're a miracle. This isn't normal."

They discharged me, but Eziah had to stay in the NICU until at least four pounds. I had a burst of energy. I was literally at the hospital every single day doing kangaroo time—skin-to-skin contact where you hold the baby against your chest.

He was so tiny he could fit in my sports bra. I would just put him in there, take pictures, talk to him, and feed him.

When I wasn't there, Lion was there. It was like I would take day shift, he would take night shift. Everybody knew Eziah. They were like, "He's so handsome, and we know he's hungry. He eats a lot."

After two weeks, the day came that we could take him home. It was the most joyous day of our lives.

After we brought Eziah home, those two weeks in the NICU were like on-the-job training. They were teaching me how to change him, when to change him, how to feed him properly as a NICU baby, how to burp him. You change the diaper right before you feed him because you know he's going to pee again right after he eats.

I learned so much, and I'm so grateful to the NICU for that preparation time.

I realized that God had ordained the job loss because I had no doctor's bills—none whatsoever. My entire pregnancy and delivery was free through social services.

I didn't have to pay for milk. They sent us free onesies, car seats, bassinets, food. We were blessed with so many things just from social services and family.

From our gender reveal, we had at least six months' worth of diapers. When we left the hospital, they loaded us up with even more. We had the baby shower as a sip-and-see after he came, and we got even more things.

I arranged to have Eziah dedicated, and we reached out to Pastor Turner again. He agreed and said to come to the church for the dedication service.

On that Sunday, right before service, Pastor Turner dedicated Eziah and gave a pledge to his godparents, grandparents, and us to make sure we're in this child's life, raising him right, being leading examples.

Following the dedication, he began his sermon. At the closing, Pastor Turner asked for salvation—if anybody wanted to give their life to Christ.

Lion stood up. Lion walked to the front and asked to have the Lord Jesus Christ come into his heart and be his Lord and Savior.

I cried. The pastor cried. My dad, my family—everybody was just like, "Whoa, that's amazing."

Eziah's dedication brought forth the salvation of his father.

Bitter, Oppressed, or Blessed

The pastor, seeing Lion from seven years old to now forty-something, standing in front of him giving his life to Christ—he was touched.

It was a full circle moment of how God had placed and lined up every piece of our lives for each other before we even knew this was going to happen.

Lion wanted to be baptized and join the church. This was God's way of saying, "Here's your church home."

We both decided to be baptized together. The Scripture came that a child will lead. We became members of the church.

Our marriage prospered. We granted forgiveness to each other and focused on raising this baby.

I ended up getting a permanent job with the state, paying way more than what I'd been earning after thirteen years with the previous company. Lion found a construction job and ran our cleaning business.

We were tremendously blessed. To this day, my son will be two, and we haven't had to buy a single piece of clothing, shoes, coats, anything for Eziah. Everyone around is always pouring into him.

God was saying, "You do not have to worry about supplying for this child. I will take care of it. He is my gift, and I'm going to take care of him."

During this time, something came upon me: "Start looking at houses. Maybe you guys can move."

I'd just started the new job, but I followed the word. Pastor Turner, who's also a realtor, found us land. We were able to move into a half-million-dollar home in 2024—almost without a job, with a brand-new baby.

We went from 1,300 square feet to 2,500 square feet, four bedrooms. God made a way during a time when interest rates were up and down. He blessed us with a 5% interest rate.

It doesn't make sense. Nothing that happens in our lives makes sense, and it's not supposed to. If it doesn't make sense, then it only means it makes God sense. That's the only way God gets the glory—when things don't make sense.

After about a year with my state job, I got "RIFed"—that's government speak for "Reduction in Force," which basically means laid off due to budget cuts. I'm literally sitting here right now in a waiting season, and God put it on my heart to tell my story, to write this book.

He literally aligned my publisher with me and told me, "You need to tell your story."

I'm like, "I'm in the middle of searching for a job."

"I'm gonna give you a little part-time job with the state, but I'm not giving you full time. You need to focus on telling this story."

Right now, as of today, I am thirty-three days late. We don't know just yet, as my story is always and continuously being written, but all I can do is laugh because I'm not scared.

I laugh at God's humor. "Are we gonna do this again? Right when I don't have a job and it doesn't make sense to have a child?"

But I'm not worried because everything will be free again. You gave us this house, so I know everything happens for a reason.

God has blessed me to see the end—not how I get there, but I can see across the street. How I'm gonna get there with no shoes, no car, no help—I'm holding my thumb up, nobody wants to give me a ride—but I can see where I'm going.

With this book, I'm understanding that sometimes you're broken for a reason. Those broken pieces are reasons you learn and grow. Just because you made so many mistakes doesn't mean you can't pick yourself back up.

God may allow things to happen to you not to break you, but

to transition you and get things out of you that you wouldn't have shared otherwise.

This book is an example because I am not a public person. I've always been the attachment, not the person out front. But God's like, "No, it's time for you to get out in front. I need you to be seen, and it's not going to be the way you think. I need you to be fully transparent because testimonies break cycles. Testimonies give restoration and generational breakthrough."

As always, my story is never ending. Right now, waiting to see what God has next. We're blessed—no disconnection notices, nothing's late. From selling the house and moving into this new house, we have emergency savings just in case.

With every downfall, with every knockout punch, we're able to get back up, and God's always making sure we're okay.

Right when I was let go from my state job, I met a young lady who became my sister in Christ. God used me to speak with her. Last week, she, her husband, and both teenage daughters were baptized at my same church with Pastor Turner.

As the pastor would say, "Easy's tree continues to grow." The child is still bringing forth more souls to Christ. It's generational blessing after blessing.

I'm learning to do what God says to do when He says to do it. I'm still working on the "when He says to do it" part, but I'm learning that He can use anybody—even the baby that probably wasn't supposed to be here, even the person that gave away their baby, even a person that's been on drugs, that's lied, that's crushed their parents—completely imperfect, sinful, terrible butterfly. He will make it into something beautiful.

The butterfly had finally learned to fly. Not just to flutter from flower to flower, but to soar above the storms that once tried to destroy her.

Ciara Briley

I dedicate this book to my Father, my Savior, the Lord. Thank You for being the greatest parent that ever existed— to give Your son and patiently watch Him die and be abused and punished for nothing He did wrong. Thank You, Jesus, for being a willing participant. Thank You, Holy Spirit, for coming upon me and letting me tell this story.

EPILOGUE
The Garden I'm Planting

Today, I'm thirty-six years old, married to my lion, raising our miracle baby in a home that God built for us. But this isn't the end of my story—it's the beginning of my ministry.

Every morning when I wake up, I think about the little girl who was told she'd end up just like her mama. I think about the teenager who fought so hard not to become her that she almost lost herself trying. I think about the young woman who ran straight into the very thing she was running from, and how even that mistake was part of God's plan.

See, I'm not writing this book just to tell my story. I'm writing it to break generational curses. To let every little girl who feels abandoned know that your beginning doesn't determine your ending. To let every woman who's made mistakes know that God's grace is bigger than your past.

I'm planting a garden now—not just for my son Eziah, but for every child who needs to know that butterflies aren't born flying. We start as caterpillars, go through seasons of darkness, fight our way through cocoons that feel like they might kill us, and emerge with wings we never knew we had.

The words "just like her mama" that were meant to break me became the very thing that made me. Because I am like my mama—I'm strong enough to make hard choices. I'm brave enough to break cycles. I'm determined enough to choose love even when it's been taken from me.

And you are too.

Your storm doesn't define you. Your cocoon doesn't confine you. Your wings are waiting.

Fly, butterfly. Fly.

HEALING BEGINS WITH A CHOICE. THIS IS YOUR INVITATION TO RISE.

FOLLOW ME

 @MRSBRILEY

 CIARA BRILEY

 @MRSBRILEY1

www.ingramcontent.com/pod-product-compliance
Lightning Source LLC
Chambersburg PA
CBHW060547190426
43201CB00050B/1904